DATE			

"DINOSAURS"
THAT SWAM AND FLEW

by David C. Knight

illustrated by
Lee J. Ames

PRENTICE-HALL, INC.
Englewood Cliffs, New Jersey

For Jennifer and Jonathan Platt

Text copyright © 1985 by David C. Knight
Illustrations copyright © 1985 by Lee J. Ames
All rights reserved. No part of this
book may be reproduced in any form or
by any means, except for the inclusion
of brief quotations in a review, without
permission in writing from the publisher.

Printed in the United States of America   •J

Prentice-Hall International, Inc., London
Prentice-Hall of Australia, Pty. Ltd., Sydney
Prentice-Hall Canada, Inc., Toronto
Prentice-Hall Hispanoamericana, S.A., Mexico
Prentice-Hall of India Private Ltd., New Delhi
Prentice-Hall of Japan, Inc., Tokyo
Prentice-Hall of Southeast Asia Pte. Ltd., Singapore
Whitehall Books Limited, Wellington, New Zealand
Editora Prentice-Hall do Brasil LTDA., Rio de Janeiro

10 9 8 7 6 5 4 3 2

Library of Congress Cataloging in Publication Data

Knight, David C.
  Dinosaurs that swam and flew.

  Summary: Text and pictures describe lesser-known
pre-historic reptiles that swam and flew.
  1. Dinosaurs—Juvenile literature. [1. Dinosaurs.
2. Prehistoric animals] I. Ames, Lee J., ill.
II. Title.
QE862.D5K56 1984   567.9'1   84-24787
ISBN 0-13-214693-2

The dinosaurs we read about in most books were land animals. They lived on the earth. Starting about 225 million years ago, generations of these amazing creatures stayed alive for over 150 million years. They finally died out, or became *extinct*, about 70 million years ago.

Some of the dinosaurs, like the giant *Brontosaurus* (*Bron-toe-saw-russ*), ate nothing but plants. Others, like the fierce *Tyrannosaurus* (*Tie-ran-oh-saw-russ*), ate nothing but meat—mostly other dinosaurs.

All of the dinosaurs were reptiles. Reptiles have back-bones and breathe air. Their bodies are covered with dry, scaly skin, and their babies are usually hatched from eggs. Reptiles are different from *mammals*, which usually have hair or fur on their bodies, and whose babies drink their mothers' milk.

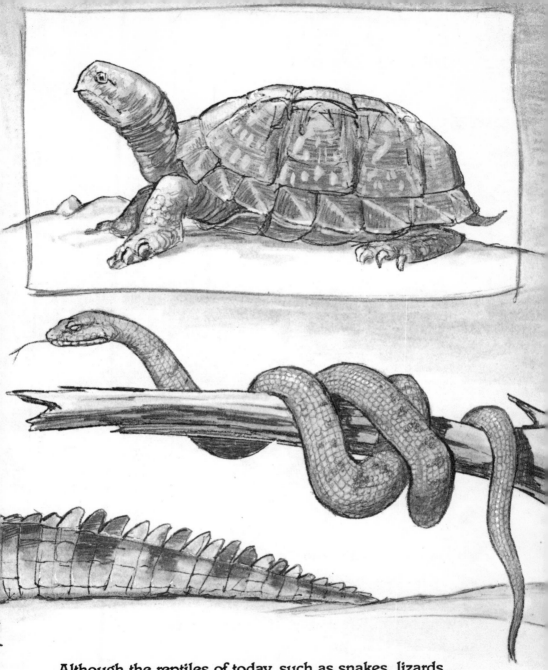

Although the reptiles of today, such as snakes, lizards, crocodiles, and turtles, are cold-blooded, some scientists now think that the dinosaurs had warm blood in their veins.

TWO THECODONTS

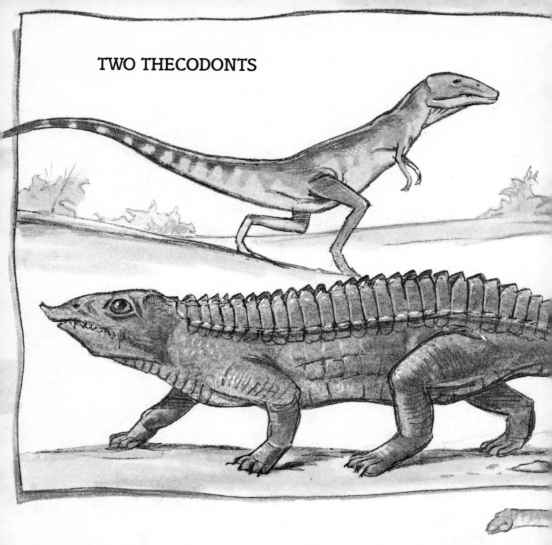

All of the land dinosaurs we read so much about had one common ancestor. These were small reptiles called *Thecodonts* (*Thee*-coe-dahnts), which measured from a few inches to 5 feet long. They appeared on the earth about 225 million years ago.

Some Thecodonts could run on their hind legs. Others walked on all four legs. Finally, after about 50 million years, the Thecodonts all died out.

But some 50 million years *before* the Thecodonts lived,
scientists think they too had a common reptile ancestor.
These were the *Cotylosaurs* (Coe-*tie*-lo-sawrs), or "stem
reptiles." Some experts believe that from them stemmed,
or developed, all the other families of ancient reptiles,
including the land dinosaurs.

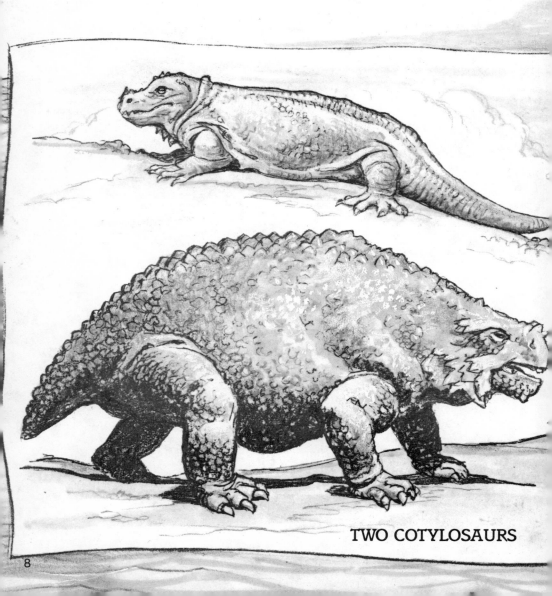

TWO COTYLOSAURS

Among those other families were reptiles that swam and later ones that flew. Although the land-dwelling reptiles are known today as the true dinosaurs, those reptiles of prehistoric seas and skies could also be called dinosaurs. The word *dinosaur* was invented in 1841 by an English scientist, Sir Richard Owen. In Greek, it simply means "terrible lizard."

Best known of the Cotylosaurs were the *Seymouria*
(*See-more-ee-ya*). They were *amphibians*, which means
they could live both on land and in the sea. About 2 feet
long, they were clumsy animals that crawled on their
bellies with legs sprawled to the side. Most lived in or
near the water, but laid their tough-shelled eggs on land.

Seymouria had sharp teeth and probably lived on smaller
animals they caught on land or in the water. The first
remains of this early reptile were found in Seymour,
Texas, in 1901. Such remains—bones, teeth, or eggs—are
called *fossils.*

One of the earliest relatives of the Cotylosaurs was a very ancient reptile called *Dimetrodon* (Die-*met*-roe-don). It lived about 240 million years ago. Dimetrodon is sometimes called the "sail reptile" because it had a 3-foot-high bony sail, or fan, on its back. Scientists think the sail collected heat from the sun, helping the cold-blooded Dimetrodon stay warm.

Dimetrodon was about 11 feet long—half of which was tail. Its name means "double-measure teeth" because its two rows of teeth were of different sizes. It never strayed far from water and fed on small animals and fish. Although Dimetrodon was cold-blooded, it was an early member of a long line that later developed into warm-blooded mammals.

Another early relative of the Cotylosaurs was *Mesosaurus*
(Mee-so-*saw*-russ). It lived at about the same time as
Dimetrodon and spent most of its time in the water. About
3 feet long, Mesosaurus lived on fish.

Mesosaurus had a very long skull, a flat-sided tail, and large numbers of thin, pointed teeth. Scientists believe this reptile lived in fresh water, not in salty seas. Fossil bones of a Mesosaurus were found several years ago in Antarctica, which was once part of an ancient continent.

200 million years ago

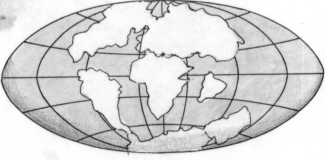

65 million years ago

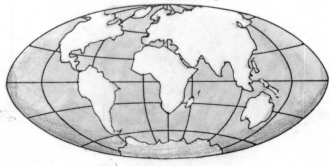

Today

Though they look like fish, these are reptiles!

After some 60 million years had gone by, the Mesosaurus line developed into the *Ichthyosaurs* (Ick-*thee*-oh-sawrs). Their name means "lizard that looks like a fish." These fishlike reptiles never left the water. They had beautiful streamlined bodies and powerful swimming muscles. Most had sharp biting teeth and they were more than a match for larger reptiles that swam in the same seas.

Mixosaurus (*Mix*-oh-saw-russ) was one of the most common early Ichthyosaurs. It reached a length of over 6 feet. Mixosaurus had a shorter snout than its later relatives and its long jaws were armed with many sharp teeth to catch fish.

Many fossil skeletons of Ichthyosaurs have been found. There is one in nearly every large natural history museum. They had very short necks, long snouts, and large round eyes protected by bony plates. Their tail fins were like those of modern sharks and their lower fins were powerful paddles that drove them swiftly through ancient oceans. The later Ichthyosaurs averaged about 12 feet in length, but some scientists think that others grew as long as 30 feet.

One type of Ichthyosaur was *Eurhinosaurus* (Yew-*hi*-no-saw-russ). It was different from other kinds because it had a short lower jaw and a very long upper jaw. Ichthyosaurs were very numerous in Europe. In the United States, their remains are found chiefly in Kansas.

These too are reptiles!

The Placodonts (*Plak*-oh-dahnts) were marine reptiles that lived over 200 million years ago. Averaging about 8 feet long, they usually fed at the bottom of prehistoric oceans. With their flat, crushing teeth and strong jaws, they could grind shellfish to bits.

One common Placodont was *Placodus* (*Plak*-oh-duss).
Its stout body, short neck, and paddlelike limbs
resembled those of a modern walrus. Its abdomen was
protected by a bony armor plate.

One of the later Thecodonts was *Protosuchus* (Pro-toe-*soo*-kuss). It is the best known ancestor of the alligators and crocodiles of today. Protosuchus measured about 3 feet in length. Its body was covered with bony plating and down the middle of its back it had a double row of plates.

Scientists think Protosuchus was probably both a good runner and a good swimmer. Its sharp, pointed teeth, made for tearing, show that it was a flesh-eater. This early reptile lived in Europe and North America about 200 million years ago.

On the sandy shores of prehistoric oceans, the first true crocodiles appeared about 180 million years ago. One of the commonest types was *Stenosaurus* (Sten-oh-*saw-russ*). It grew to between 12 and 20 feet in length.

Stenosaurus's five-toed forelimbs were much smaller than its four-toed hind limbs. Both pairs of feet were webbed and the first three toes had pointed claws for clutching and walking on land. These reptiles were very plentiful in the seas of Europe, North Africa, and America.

Very well suited to life in ancient seas was *Nothosaurus* (No-tho-*saw*-russ). This marine reptile lived at the same time as the Placodonts and Ichthyosaurs. Scientists believe it to be the ancestor of the *Plesiosaurs* (*Pleez-ee-oh-sawrs*), described in the next pages.

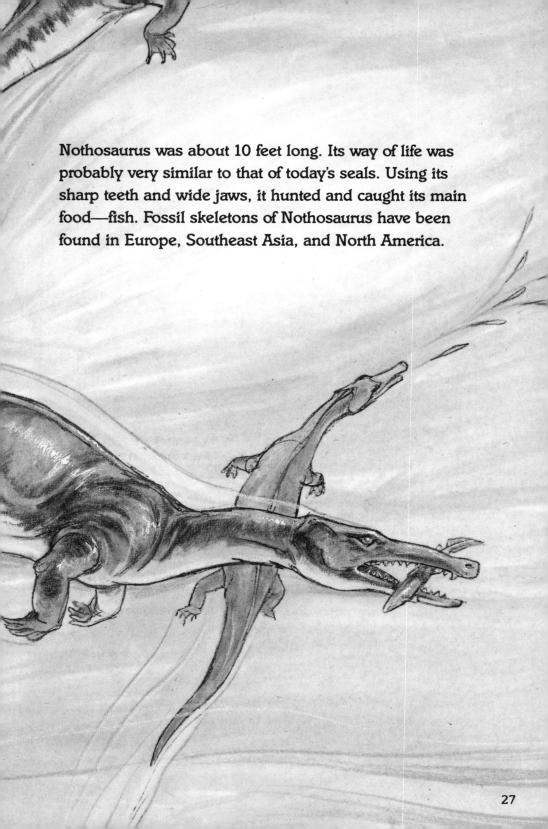

Nothosaurus was about 10 feet long. Its way of life was probably very similar to that of today's seals. Using its sharp teeth and wide jaws, it hunted and caught its main food—fish. Fossil skeletons of Nothosaurus have been found in Europe, Southeast Asia, and North America.

After living on land for over 70 million years, some reptiles returned to the oceans. One important group of these were the *Plesiosaurs.* With their long, swanlike necks and jagged teeth, they were the dragons of the prehistoric seas. Their great swimming power was in their four oarlike flippers, which had once been their feet on land. There were many kinds and sizes of these reptiles.

Making up one large branch of the Plesiosaurs was *Peloneustes* (Peh-lon-*ess*-teez). These marine reptiles had short necks, thick bodies, and rather large skulls. Peloneustes was about 10 feet long and fed on fish.

One of the commonest Plesiosaurs was *Plesiosaurus* (*Pleez-ee-oh-saw-russ*). It had a long, snaky neck, a short tail, and a barrel-shaped body. It averaged between 10 and 13 feet. The reptile's flippers were strong enough to allow it to come out of the water and move about on land, as seals do today.

But much of the time Plesiosaurus spent in the water, where it could either catch fish on the surface or dive for them. With its long, strong paddles, Plesiosaurus could row itself through the water very quickly.

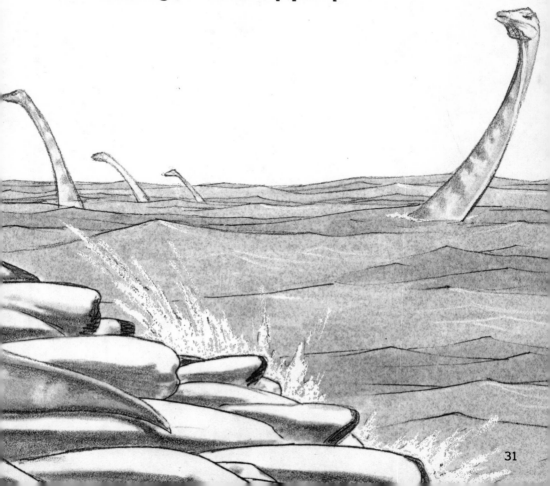

Another member of the Plesiosaur family was *Cryptocleidus* (Krip-toe-*klie*-duss). It used its long, flexible neck to snatch its food from passing schools of fish. This marine reptile was about 11 feet long.

The eyes of Plesiosaurs were located at the sides of their heads and were quite large. The nostrils through which they breathed were just in front of their eyes. Their pointed teeth were set in sockets at the edge of their jawbones.

The king of the Plesiosaurs was *Elasmosaurus* (Ee-laz-moe-saw-russ). This giant marine reptile was some 44 feet long. Some experts insist that these creatures grew to 60 feet! They lived in the ancient seas of North America about 80 million years ago.

Elasmosaurus had the longest neck of all the Plesiosaurs. It was almost twice the length of its body. The neck contained large numbers of *vertebrae*—bone segments—permitting Elasmosaurus to swing its head in a complete circle. In this way, it could spear plenty of fish far away from its body.

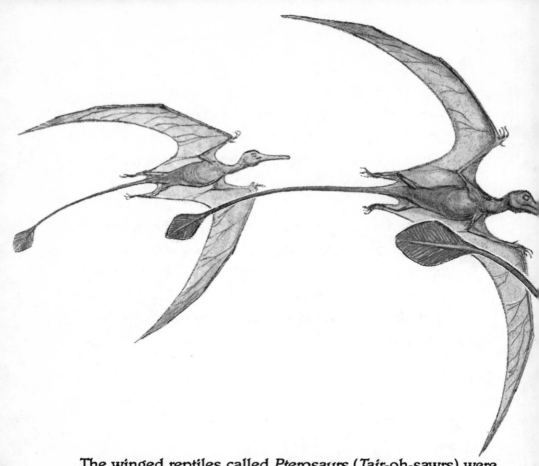

The winged reptiles called *Pterosaurs* (*Tair*-oh-sawrs) were the first *vertebrates*—creatures with backbones—to conquer the air. One of the earliest of these was *Rhamphorhynchus* (Ram-for-*ink*-uss). Its name means "beak-snouted." It developed from Thecodont ancestors and lived about 150 million years ago.

Rhamphorhyncus had a wingspan of up to 6 feet, a long skull and neck, and a short body about 20 inches long. Its long, thin tail ended in a diamond-shaped flap of skin. The fourth finger of its forelimbs was extremely long and supported its leathery wings. Rhamphorhynchus could glide for short distances, scoop up food from the sea, then land on cliffs where it made its home.

Pterosaurs, like birds, had hollow bones filled with air. This made their bodies lighter for flight. The winged reptiles called *Pterodactyls* (Tair-oh-*dak*-tiles) had short tails, wide wings, and long beak-like jaws with sharp teeth. No one knows for sure just how they flew; probably they simply glided and soared.

The Pterodactyls lived in flocks and ate insects and fish. They too supported their wings from the long fourth fingers of the forelimbs. Pterodactyls lived near the shores of prehistoric seas and may have slept hanging from tree branches by their feet, like bats.

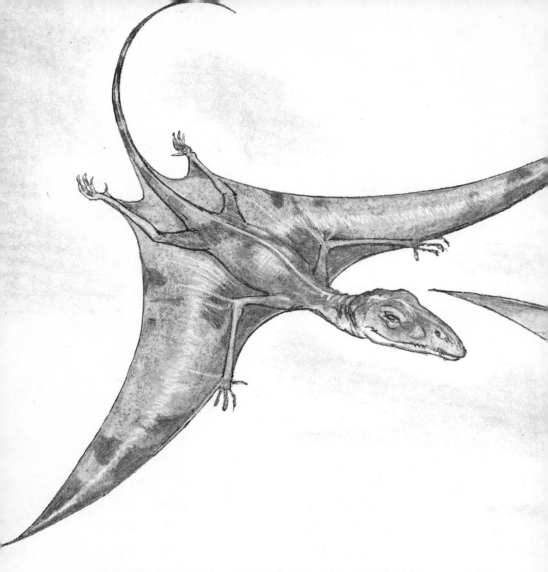

Another member of the Pterosaur family was
Dimorphodon (Die-*morf*-oh-don). It was a little over 4 feet
long, including its thin tail. Dimorphodon had strong
limbs and a short, lightly-built body. Scientists think it
was a flesh-eating animal which fed on small animals
and fish.

The striking feature about Dimorphodon was its bulky but lightly built skull. It was about 9 inches long and its jaws were filled with pointed teeth. This flying reptile had a wingspan of about 5 feet.

The largest winged reptile of all was *Pteranodon* (Tair-an-oh-don). Its name means "winged, but without teeth." It had a wingspan of over 25 feet, a bony crest on its head, and a long, sharp bill. Even though this beaklike mouth was toothless, it was well made to catch fish and small marine animals.

Because of its large size and wingspread, it is hard to see how Pteranodon could have taken to the air. Some experts think it started off on a long glide from a cliff or high tree, caught its food, and then soared upward again on wind currents.

Because Pteranodon's legs were probably too weak to support its body, it may have dropped food to its babies from the air. The tall crest on its head may have acted as a rudder to hold it steady in flight and help it make turns. Several well-preserved skeletons of Pteranodon have been taken from rocks in Kansas.

Most fossil remains of Pterosaurs have been found in places scientists know were once covered with water. Apparently they never wandered far from ancient seas and lakes, which provided them with food. They would also have needed the wind coming off the water to make their take-offs.

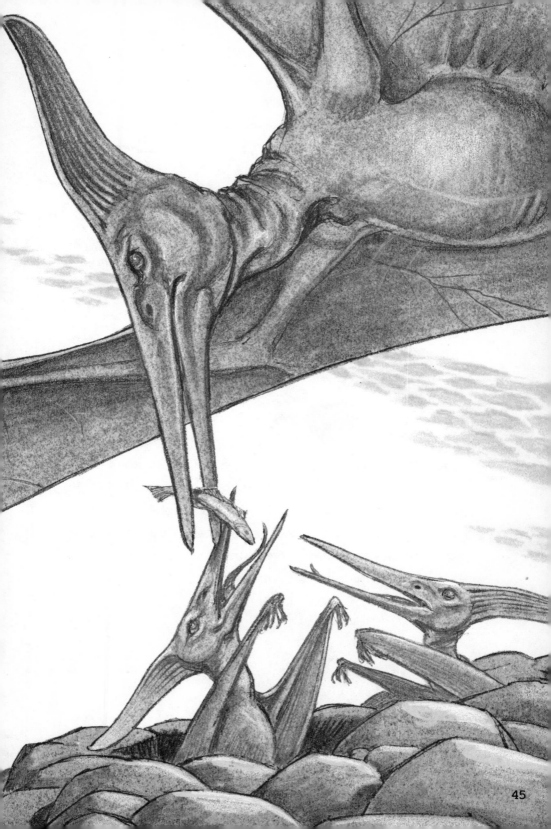

45

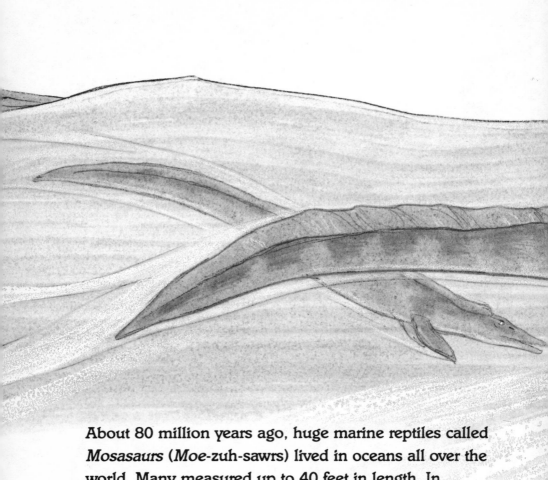

About 80 million years ago, huge marine reptiles called
Mosasaurs (*Moe*-zuh-sawrs) lived in oceans all over the
world. Many measured up to 40 feet in length. In
America, the great sea that once covered many western
states must have been alive with Mosasaurs. Just about
every large museum has one on display.

Mosasaur means "reptile from the Meuse," the river in Europe along which its remains were first found. These fierce sea reptiles were completely adapted to life in the water. With their powerful tails and flippers, they could churn swiftly through the ocean in search of prey.

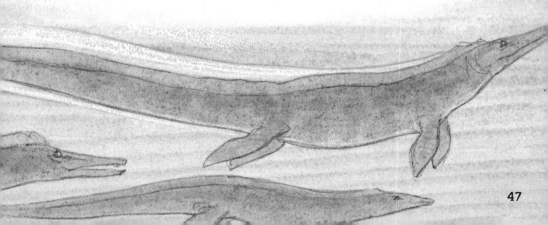

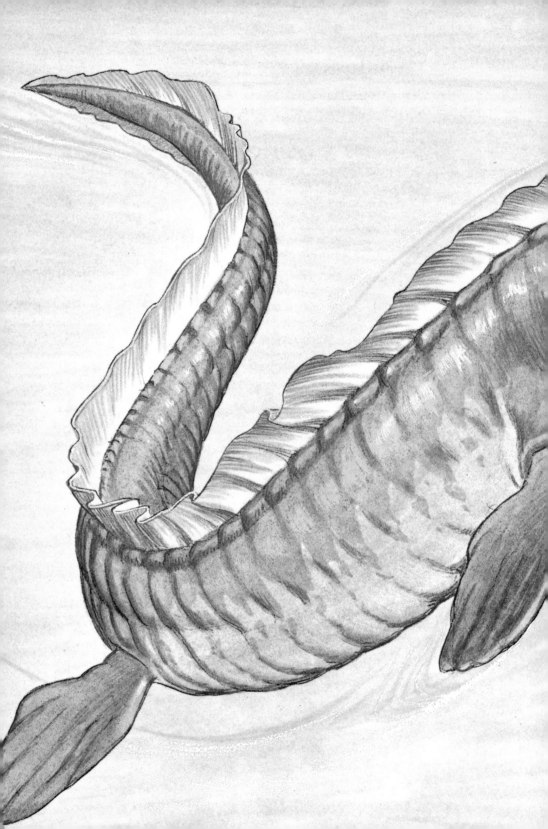

Largest and fiercest of the Mosasaurs was *Tylosaurus* (Tie-lo-*saw*-russ). It had a skull over 3 feet long and enormous jaws filled with sharklike teeth. Its powerful flat tail, lashing from side to side, was its main swimming organ.

The Mosasaurs had nostrils located in the tops of their skulls for breathing. Although they were completely sea-going reptiles, the Mosasaurs were as long and weighed as much as many land-dwelling dinosaurs.

In the ancient seas in which they both lived, such
marine giants as Tylosaurus and Elasmosaurus
certainly must have met at times—and probably
threatened each other. Perhaps one had strayed into
another's fishing grounds. Or possibly both were
chasing the same school of fish.

Elasmosaurus, with its long, swinging neck, may have
snapped viciously at Tylosaurus's head and body to
warn it away. But it is doubtful that Elasmosaurus would
have tried to battle Tylosaurus to the death. Tylosaurus's
savage toothed jaws had the power to wrench the
Plesiosaur's slender neck from its body.

Also living together with Mosasaurs and Plesiosaurs in prehistoric seas was the giant turtle *Archelon* (Ar-kell-on). The largest turtle ever known, it was 12 feet long and 11 feet wide. It weighed between 2 and 3 tons. Archelon's name means "ruler turtle," referring to its enormous size.

Like modern turtles, Archelon was helpless out of water
on ancient beaches. Its short legs could not have lifted its
heavy body down to the water again. It had to wait for the
tide to come back in so it could float free. Its shell wasn't
solid but had openings covered with leathery hide. This
made it lighter and able to swim better.

The largest of all the short-necked Plesiosaurs was the massive *Kronosaurus* (Kroe-no-*saw*-russ). A fossil skeleton of this monster was unearthed in Australia which measures 42 feet. Like other Plesiosaurs, it developed a hard rib cage to protect its underside from attack by enemies.

Kronosaurus had a 9-foot head and large limbs like paddles. It was a fast-diving flesh-eater with huge jaws that could grab and kill fish and other marine creatures. Scientists think it may have even fed on fellow Plesiosaurs.

The earliest primitive bird was *Archaeopteryx* (Ark-ee-op-ter-ix). About as big as a crow, it was closely related to reptile ancestors. Its jaws were covered with scales and contained small teeth. This ancestor of modern birds probably ate worms, berries, and insects.

Archaeopteryx was warm-blooded and its once-fringed scales had developed into feathers. These features gave it two advantages over true reptiles: it was more active and could withstand changing temperatures better. Because its wing muscles were weak, *Archaeopteryx* could not make long flights. But it had learned to flap its wings, as birds do today.

About 70 million years ago, the Age of Reptiles came to an end (although this process took several thousands of years). All of the land dinosaurs died out. Scientists still aren't sure why this happened, but there are many theories. Some great disaster, like exploding volcanoes or disease, may have wiped them out. Or the climate may have become too hot or too cold for the dinosaurs to survive.

About this same time, the still-surviving marine and flying reptiles also died out. All members of the once-mighty swimming families—the Ichthyosaurs and Plesiosaurs—perished. So did the winged reptiles—the soaring, gliding Pterosaurs. Only a few of the reptile lines survived to develop into today's snakes, lizards, turtles, alligators, crocodiles—and birds.

In recent years, scientists have come up with new theories about why the Age of Reptiles ended so suddenly. One is that a star exploded relatively near the earth, sending radiation to our planet. When this radiation was absorbed into the atmosphere, it may have formed ice crystals which blocked out the warm rays of the sun. The resulting cold spell may have killed off the dinosaurs, including the marine and winged reptiles.

Another theory is that the earth was struck by a passing *asteroid,* one of many thousands of tiny planets in our solar system. The tremendous impact may have stirred up clouds of poisonous dust in the atmosphere. The dust would have gotten into the food the dinosaurs ate, the air they breathed, and the seas in which they swam, killing them off in a relatively short time. The dust may also have cooled the atmosphere, lowered the temperature, and killed off the dinosaurs that way.

The truth is, it's still a mystery why the last reptiles of the land, sea, and air died out at about the same period in the earth's history. Somehow conditions on earth changed drastically. The reptiles couldn't change with them—and so they became extinct.

Some Museums in Which Remains of Marine and Flying Reptiles Can Be Seen

CANADA

Ontario: National Museum of Natural Sciences, Ottawa
Ontario: Royal Ontario Museum, Toronto

UNITED STATES

California: Museum of Paleontology, University of
California, Berkeley
Colorado: Denver Museum of Natural History, Denver
Connecticut: Peabody Museum of Natural History, Yale
University, New Haven
District of Columbia: Smithsonian Institution, Museum of
Natural History, Washington
Illinois: Field Museum of Natural History, Chicago
Kansas: University of Kansas Museum, Lawrence
Massachusetts: Amherst College Museum, Amherst
Museum of Comparative Zoology, Harvard
University, Cambridge

Michigan: Museum of Paleontology, University of
Michigan, Ann Arbor
Nebraska: University of Nebraska State Museum, Lincoln
New Jersey: Museum of Natural History, Princeton
University, Princeton
New York: American Museum of Natural History,
New York City
Ohio: Cleveland Museum of Natural History, Cleveland
Oklahoma: Stovall Museum, University of Oklahoma,
Norman
Pennsylvania: Academy of Natural Sciences, Philadelphia
Carnegie Museum, Carnegie Institute, Pittsburgh
Texas: Texas Memorial Museum, Austin
El Paso Centennial Museum, University of Texas,
El Paso
Utah: Utah Museum of Natural History, University of
Utah, Salt Lake City
Dinosaur National Monument, Summit Valley

Index